THE
FABULOUS
LOST &
FOUND

AND THE LITTLE GERMAN MOUSE

WRITTEN BY MARK PALLIS
ILLUSTRATED BY PETER BAYNTON

NEU WESTEND
— PRESS —

For Emily and Lucy. Legends! - MP

For Hannah and Skye - PB

THE FABULOUS LOST & FOUND AND THE LITTLE GERMAN MOUSE
Copyright text © 2020 Mark Pallis and Copyright images © 2020 Peter Baynton

First Printing, 2020
ISBN: 978-1-913595-00-5
NeuWestendPress.com

THE FABULOUS LOST & FOUND

AND THE LITTLE GERMAN MOUSE

WRITTEN BY MARK PALLIS
ILLUSTRATED BY PETER BAYNTON

NEU WESTEND
— PRESS —

In the middle of the big city is a tiny
yellow building. If anyone loses anything, this is
where it ends up.

It is called the Lost and Found.

Mr and Mrs Frog keep everything safe, hoping that someday every lost watch and bag and phone and toy and shoe and cheesegrater will find its owner again.

But the shop is very small. And there are so many lost things. It is all quite a squeeze, but still, it's fabulous.

One sunny day, a little mouse walked in.

"Welcome," said Mrs Frog. "What have you lost?"

"Ich habe meine Pudelmütze verloren," said the mouse.

Mr and Mrs Frog could not speak German. They had no idea what the little mouse was saying.

What shall we do? they wondered.

Maybe she's lost an umbrella. Everyone loses an umbrella at least twice, thought Mr Frog.

"Have you lost this?" asked Mr Frog.

"Ein Regenschirm? Nein," replied the mouse.

Then Mrs Frog remembered something that had been handed in a few months ago...

"Is this yours?" Mrs Frog asked, holding up a chunk of cheese.

"Käse? Nein. Er stinkt!" said the mouse.

"Time to put that cheese in the bin dear," said Mr Frog.

"Maybe the word 'Pudelmütze' means coat," said Mr Frog.

"Now where did I put that nice yellow one?"

"Got it!" said Mr Frog.

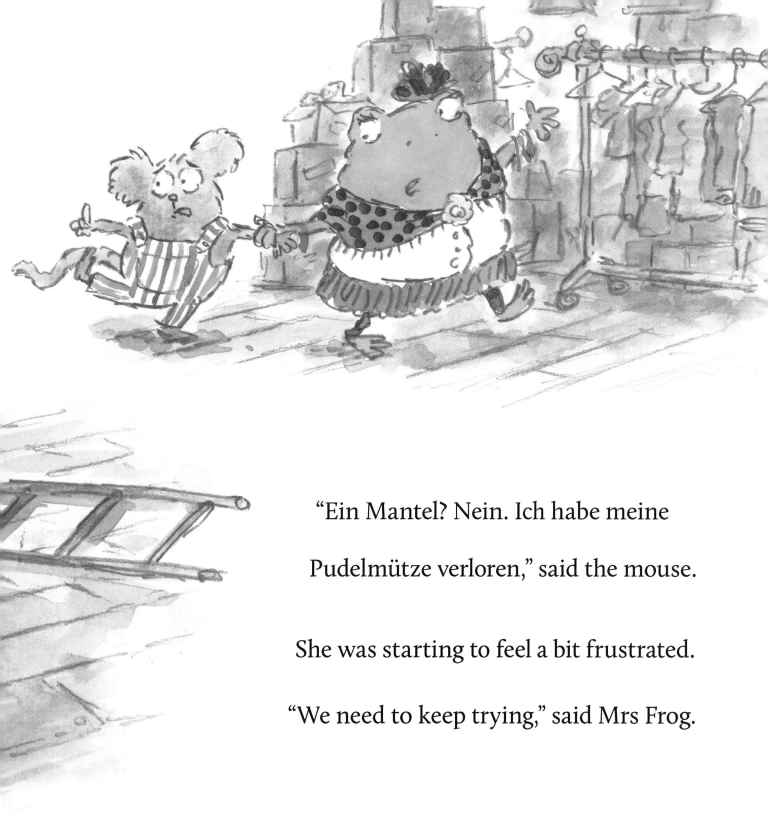

"Ein Mantel? Nein. Ich habe meine Pudelmütze verloren," said the mouse.

She was starting to feel a bit frustrated.

"We need to keep trying," said Mrs Frog.

Kein Schal.

Keine Hose.

Kein Pulli.

Keine Sonnenbrille.

Keine Schuhe.

"Ich habe meine Pudelmütze
verloren," said the mouse.

Nicht zwei Fahrräder.

Kein Computer.

Nicht drei Bücher.

Nicht vier Bananen.

Nicht fünf Schlüssel.

It was no good. A fat wet tear rolled
down the mouse's cheek.

"How about a nice cup of tea?" asked Mrs Frog kindly.

"Ich liebe Tee. Danke," replied the mouse. They sat together, sipping their tea and all feeling a bit sad.

Suddenly, the mouse realised she could try pointing.

"Pudelmütze!" she said.

"I've got it!" exclaimed Mrs Frog, leaping up.

"A wig of course!" said Mrs Frog.

"Keine Perücke," said the mouse.

Nicht rot.

Nicht blond.

Nicht braun.

Nicht bunt.

Nicht grün.

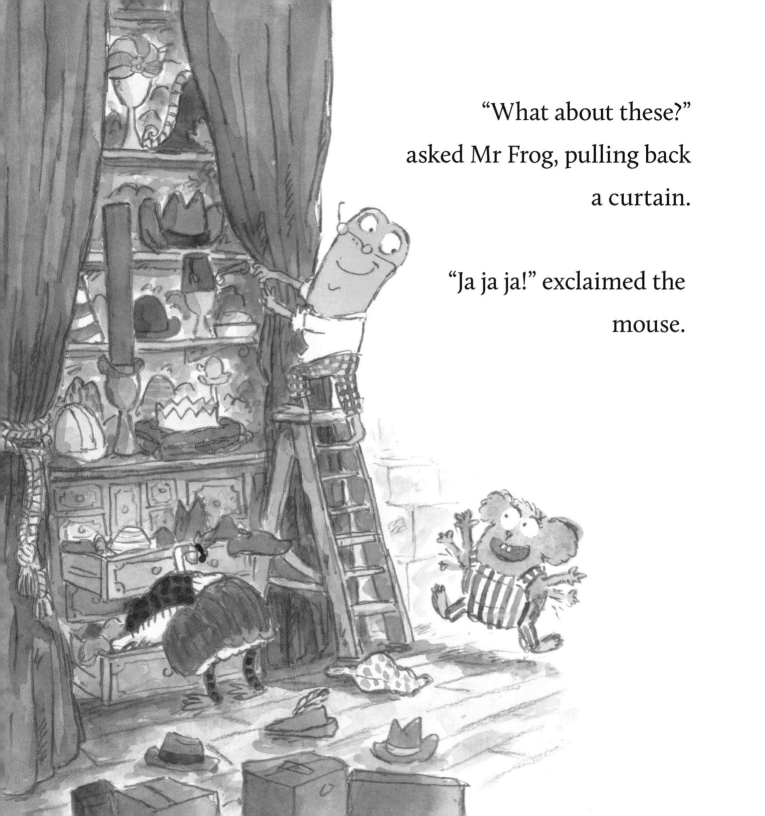

"What about these?" asked Mr Frog, pulling back a curtain.

"Ja ja ja!" exclaimed the mouse.

Zu hoch.

Zu klein.

Zu groß.

Zu eng.

"One hat left," said Mrs Frog, reaching all the way to the back of the cupboard.

"It couldn't be this old thing, could it?"

"Meine Pudelmütze! Ich habe meine Pudelmütze gefunden!

Vielen Dank," said the mouse.

"Ah, so 'Pudelmütze' means bobble hat. Wonderful!"
Mr and Mrs Frog smiled.

And just like that, the mouse found her hat.

"Tschüss," she said, as she skipped away.
"Tschüss," replied Mr and Mrs Frog.

"I wonder who will come tomorrow?" said Mr Frog.
Mrs Frog put her arm around him.

"I don't know," she replied, giving him a squeeze,
"but whoever it is, we'll do our best to help."

LEARNING TO LOVE LANGUAGES

An additional language opens a child's mind, broadens their horizons and enriches their emotional life. Research has shown that the time between a child's birth and their sixth or seventh birthday is a "golden period" when they are most receptive to new languages. This is because they have an in-built ability to distinguish the sounds they hear and make sense of them. The Story-powered Language Learning Method taps into these natural abilities.

HOW THE STORY-POWERED LANGUAGE LEARNING METHOD WORKS

We create an emotionally engaging and funny story for children and adults to enjoy together, just like any other picture book. Studies show that social interaction, like enjoying a book together, is critical in language learning.

Through the story, we introduce a relatable character who speaks only in the new language. This helps build empathy and a positive attitude towards people who speak different languages. These are both important aspects in laying the foundations for lasting language acquisition in a child's life.

As the story progresses, the child naturally works with the characters to discover the meaning of a wide range of fun new words. Strategic use of humour ensures that this subconscious learning is rewarded with laughter; the child feels good and the first seeds of a lifelong love of languages are sown.

For more information and free downloads visit www.neuwestendpress.com

ALL THE BEAUTIFUL GERMAN WORDS AND PHRASES FROM OUR STORY

Ich habe meine Pudelmütze verloren	I've lost my bobble hat
ein Regenschirm	an umbrella
käse	cheese
er stinkt	it stinks
ein Mantel	a coat
Schal	scarf
Hose	trousers
Sonnenbrille	sunglasses
Pulli	sweater
Schuhe	shoes
eins	one
zwei	two
drei	three
vier	four
fünf	five
Computer	computer
Bücher	books
Schlüssel	key
Bananen	bananas
Fahrräder	bicycles
Ich liebe Tee	I love tea
danke	thank you
Vielen Dank	thanks very much
Perücke	wig

German	English
rot	red
blond	blond
braun	brown
grün	green
bunt	multicoloured
nein	no
ja	yes
zu hoch	too tall
zu groß	too big
zu klein	too small
zu eng	too tight
Ich habe meine Pudelmütze gefunden	I've found my bobble hat
Tschüss	bye

THE WORLD OF
THE FABULOUS LOST & FOUND

THIS STORY IS ALSO AVAILABLE IN...

FRENCH
SPANISH
ITALIAN
CZECH
KOREAN
WELSH
GREEK
HEBREW
SWEDISH
POLISH
SLOVAKIAN
VIETNAMESE
LATIN
PORTUGUESE

...AND MANY MORE LANGUAGES!

ENJOYED IT?
WRITE A REVIEW AND
LET US KNOW!

@MARK_PALLIS ON TWITTER
WWW.MARKPALLIS.COM

@PETERBAYNTON ON INSTAGRAM
WWW.PETERBAYNTON.COM

Printed in Great Britain
by Amazon